D1456576

CONTINENTS

NORTH AMERICA

Cass R. Sandak

RSVP

RAINTREE
STECK-VAUGHN
PUBLISHERS
The Steck-Vaughn Company

Austin, Texas

CONTINENTS

AFRICA   EUROPE

ANTARCTICA   NORTH AMERICA

ASIA   SOUTH AMERICA

AUSTRALIA & OCEANIA

Published by Raintree Steck-Vaughn Publishers, an imprint of Steck-Vaughn Company

Library of Congress Cataloging-in-Publication Data
Sandak, Cass R.
North America / Cass R. Sandak.
    p.   cm.—(Continents)
Includes bibliographical references and index.
Summary: Examines the geography, history, economy, and culture of the North American continent.
ISBN 0-8172-4780-7
1. North America—Juvenile literature.
[1. North America.]
I. Title. II. Series: Continents (Austin, TX).
E38.5.S36 1998
917—dc21   97-5819

Printed in Italy. Bound in the United States.
1 2 3 4 5 6 7 8 9 0 02 01 00 99 98

Contents page: Harvesting eggplants on a farm in Texas

Picture Acknowledgments
Bryan and Cherry Alexander 12 top, 35 bottom; Camera Press 37; Ecoscene 17 top; Eye Ubiquitous 11, 17 bottom, 26, 28, 30 top, 31 top, 39 top, 42 top; Robert Harding 10, 23, 24, 32 bottom, 35 top; Impact Photos 15 top (Richard McCraig), 22 (D.Palmer), 25 bottom (S.Benbow), 29 (J.Cole), 34 (S.Dorantes), 36 bottom (B.Harris); Panos Pictures 27 top (A.le Garomeur); Eddie Parker 27 bottom, 43; Pictor 12 bottom, 25 top; Popperfoto 15 bottom, 41 top, 41 bottom (C.Pillitz); Rex features 36 top, 40; South American Pictures 19, 30 bottom (R.Francis), 31 bottom (R,Francis), 38 (P.Dixon); Still Pictures 32 top (D.Dancer); Topham 20 bottom; Wayland Picture Library 18, 20 top, 21; Zefa 16.

CONTENTS

NORTH AMERICA BY COUNTRY

CANADA

Canada is the largest country in the Western Hemisphere, and after Russia, it is the second largest country in area in the world. Despite its size, Canada ranks only 31st in population. In fact, it is one of the least densely populated countries in the world. On average, there is only about 1 person per square mile, and 80 percent of Canadians live within 200 mi. of the Canada-U.S. border. Vast areas of the north are virtually uninhabited. Some 62 percent of all Canadians live in the provinces of Quebec and Ontario.

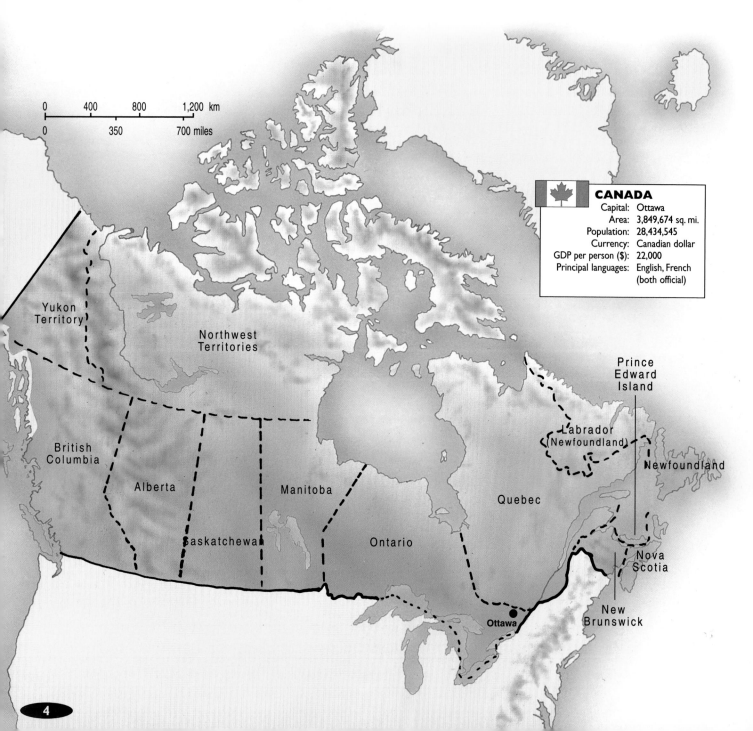

CANADA

Capital:	Ottawa
Area:	3,849,674 sq. mi.
Population:	28,434,545
Currency:	Canadian dollar
GDP per person ($):	22,000
Principal languages:	English, French (both official)

0   400   800   1,200 km

0   350   700 miles

Yukon Territory

Northwest Territories

British Columbia

Alberta

Saskatchewan

Manitoba

Ontario

Quebec

Labrador (Newfoundland)

Prince Edward Island

Newfoundland

Nova Scotia

New Brunswick

Ottawa

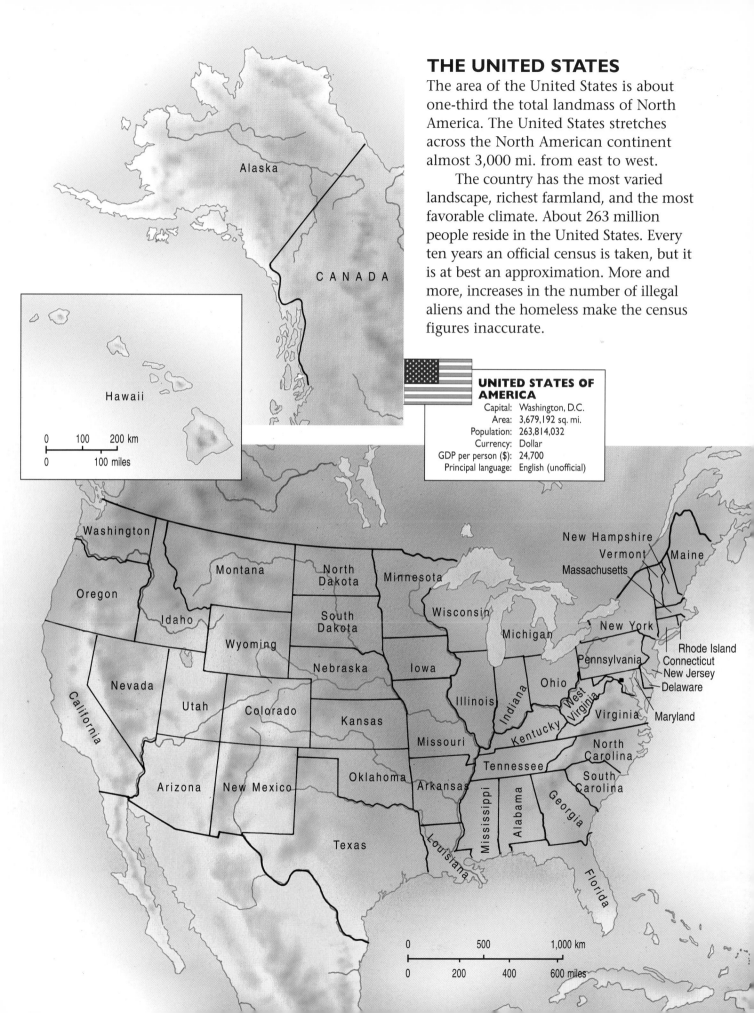

THE UNITED STATES

The area of the United States is about one-third the total landmass of North America. The United States stretches across the North American continent almost 3,000 mi. from east to west.

The country has the most varied landscape, richest farmland, and the most favorable climate. About 263 million people reside in the United States. Every ten years an official census is taken, but it is at best an approximation. More and more, increases in the number of illegal aliens and the homeless make the census figures inaccurate.

UNITED STATES OF AMERICA
Capital: Washington, D.C.
Area: 3,679,192 sq. mi.
Population: 263,814,032
Currency: Dollar
GDP per person ($): 24,700
Principal language: English (unofficial)

Alaska

CANADA

Hawaii

0   100   200 km
0   100 miles

Washington
Oregon
Idaho
Montana
North Dakota
South Dakota
Minnesota
Wisconsin
Michigan
New Hampshire
Vermont
Maine
Massachusetts
New York
Nevada
Utah
Wyoming
Nebraska
Iowa
Illinois
Indiana
Ohio
Pennsylvania
Rhode Island
Connecticut
New Jersey
Delaware
California
Colorado
Kansas
Missouri
Kentucky
West Virginia
Virginia
Maryland
Arizona
New Mexico
Oklahoma
Arkansas
Tennessee
North Carolina
South Carolina
Mississippi
Alabama
Georgia
Texas
Louisiana
Florida

0   500   1,000 km
0   200   400   600 miles

MEXICO

The official name of Mexico is the Estados Unidos Mexicanos, or the United Mexican States. The third largest country in North America is made up of 31 states and a federal district that includes Mexico City, the nation's capital and one of the world's largest cities. With an estimated 20 million people, Mexico City contains between 20 and 25 percent of Mexico's entire population, which is estimated to be more than 93 million. Mexico is the largest Spanish-speaking country in the world. The country is one and a half times the size of the state of Alaska and is considerably wider in the north than in the south. Its border with the United States is about 1,500 mi. across.

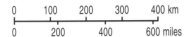

MEXICO

Capital:	Mexico City
Area:	756,066 sq. mi.
Population:	93,985,848
Currency:	New Peso
GDP per person ($):	8,200
Principal languages:	Spanish (official), Amerindian languages

1 Federal District
2 Mexico
3 Tlaxcala
4 Puebla
5 Morelos
6 Hidalgo
7 Querétaro
8 Guanajuato
9 Aguas Calientes

CENTRAL AMERICA

Central America consists of seven countries. These form a slender isthmus that stretches southward from the border of Mexico through the Panama Canal Zone on to the northernmost tip of South America. Much of the land is mountainous, and hidden in the mountains are many volcanoes, some of which are still active. Bananas, coffee, and cacao are the principal agricultural products. Gold and silver are also mined.

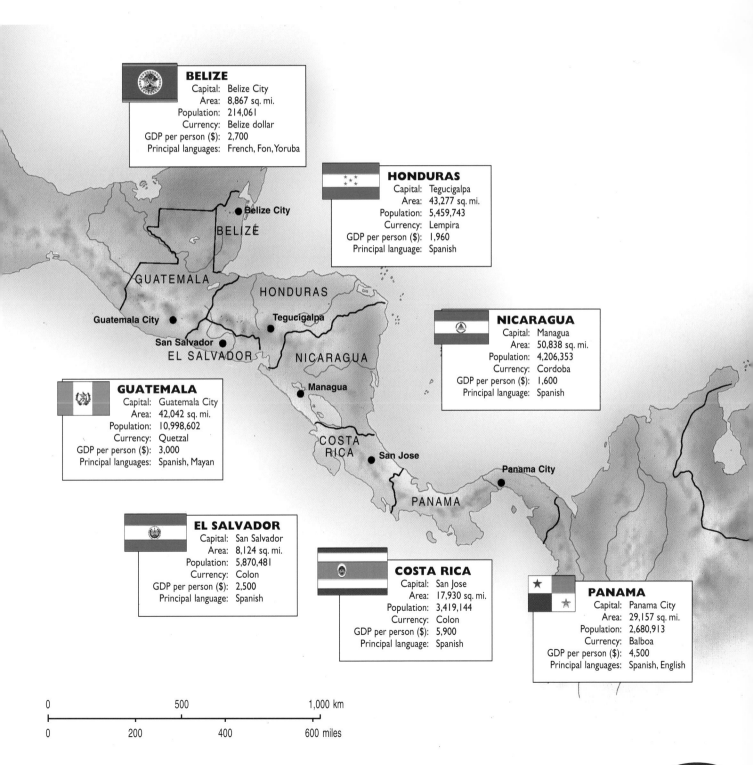

BELIZE
Capital: Belize City
Area: 8,867 sq. mi.
Population: 214,061
Currency: Belize dollar
GDP per person ($): 2,700
Principal languages: French, Fon, Yoruba

HONDURAS
Capital: Tegucigalpa
Area: 43,277 sq. mi.
Population: 5,459,743
Currency: Lempira
GDP per person ($): 1,960
Principal language: Spanish

NICARAGUA
Capital: Managua
Area: 50,838 sq. mi.
Population: 4,206,353
Currency: Cordoba
GDP per person ($): 1,600
Principal language: Spanish

GUATEMALA
Capital: Guatemala City
Area: 42,042 sq. mi.
Population: 10,998,602
Currency: Quetzal
GDP per person ($): 3,000
Principal languages: Spanish, Mayan

EL SALVADOR
Capital: San Salvador
Area: 8,124 sq. mi.
Population: 5,870,481
Currency: Colon
GDP per person ($): 2,500
Principal language: Spanish

COSTA RICA
Capital: San Jose
Area: 17,930 sq. mi.
Population: 3,419,144
Currency: Colon
GDP per person ($): 5,900
Principal language: Spanish

PANAMA
Capital: Panama City
Area: 29,157 sq. mi.
Population: 2,680,913
Currency: Balboa
GDP per person ($): 4,500
Principal languages: Spanish, English

0   500   1,000 km

0   200   400   600 miles

ISLANDS OF THE CARIBBEAN

The islands of the Caribbean Sea—a branch of the central
Atlantic covering roughly 1.4 million sq. mi.—are known as the
West Indies. The Caribbean Sea was named after the Carib
Indians, native inhabitants of the Lesser Antilles. The Caribs
probably came from South America, and when they got to the
islands, they found a group of people who had already been there
for many centuries, the Arawak.

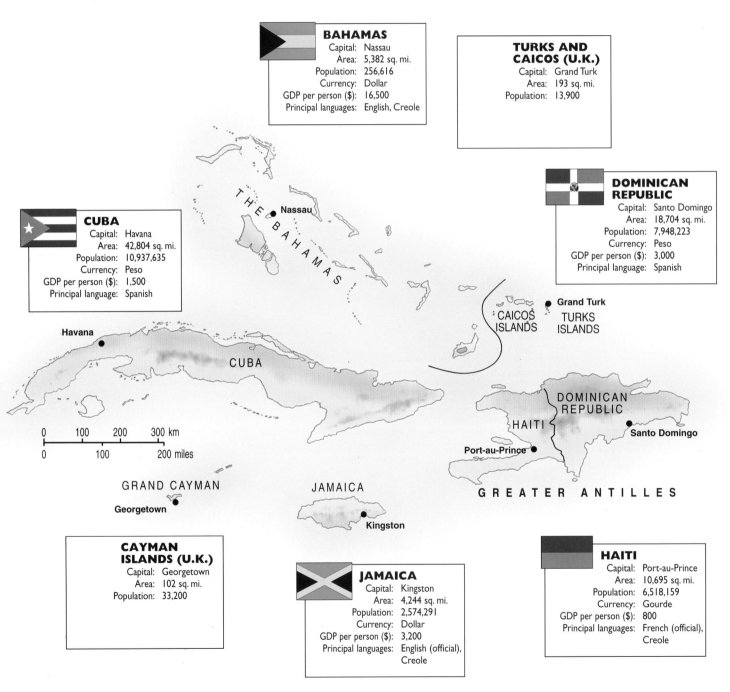

BAHAMAS
Capital: Nassau
Area: 5,382 sq. mi.
Population: 256,616
Currency: Dollar
GDP per person ($): 16,500
Principal languages: English, Creole

TURKS AND CAICOS (U.K.)
Capital: Grand Turk
Area: 193 sq. mi.
Population: 13,900

DOMINICAN REPUBLIC
Capital: Santo Domingo
Area: 18,704 sq. mi.
Population: 7,948,223
Currency: Peso
GDP per person ($): 3,000
Principal language: Spanish

CUBA
Capital: Havana
Area: 42,804 sq. mi.
Population: 10,937,635
Currency: Peso
GDP per person ($): 1,500
Principal language: Spanish

CAYMAN ISLANDS (U.K.)
Capital: Georgetown
Area: 102 sq. mi.
Population: 33,200

JAMAICA
Capital: Kingston
Area: 4,244 sq. mi.
Population: 2,574,291
Currency: Dollar
GDP per person ($): 3,200
Principal languages: English (official), Creole

HAITI
Capital: Port-au-Prince
Area: 10,695 sq. mi.
Population: 6,518,159
Currency: Gourde
GDP per person ($): 800
Principal languages: French (official), Creole

PUERTO RICO (U.S.)

Capital: San Juan
Area: 3,492 sq. mi.
Population: 3,801,977
Currency: Dollar
GDP per person ($): 6,360 (1992)
Principal languages: English, Spanish (joint)

ANTIGUA AND BARBUDA

Capital: St. John's
Area: 170 sq. mi.
Population: 65,176
Currency: Caribbean dollar
GDP per person ($): 5,800
Principal language: English

DOMINICA

Capital: Roseau
Area: 290 sq. mi.
Population: 82,608
Currency: East Caribbean dollar
GDP per person ($): 3,000
Principal language: Spanish

Roadtown
VIRGIN ISLANDS
Charlotte Amalie

St. KITTS & NEVIS

ANTIGUA & BARBUDA

San Juan

PUERTO RICO

St. John's

Basseterre

GUADELOUPE

L E S S E R A N T I L L E S

Pointe-a-Pitre

DOMINICA

Roseau

MAIN CARIBBEAN TERRITORIES

These territories are administered by other countries but control many aspects of their own governments:

Territory	Capital:	Administered by:
Bermuda	Hamilton	Great Britain
Curacao	Willemstad	Netherlands
Guadeloupe	Pointe-a-Pitre	France
Martinique	Fort-de-France	France
St. Kitts & Nevis	Basseterre	Great Britain
Virgin Islands (British)	Roadtown	Great Britain
Virgin Islands (U.S.)	Charlotte-Amalie	United States

MARTINIQUE

Fort-de-France

ST. LUCIA

Capital: Castries
Area: 238 sq. mi.
Population: 156,050
Currency: East Caribbean dollar
GDP per person ($): 2,000
Principal language: English

ST. VINCENT AND THE GRENADINES

Capital: Kingstown
Area: 150 sq. mi.
Population: 117,580
Currency: East Caribbean dollar
GDP per person ($): 2,000
Principal languages: English, French

Castries
St. LUCIA

BARBADOS

Bridgetown

Kingstown
St. VINCENT

BARBADOS

Capital: Bridgetown
Area: 166 sq. mi.
Population: 256,395
Currency: Dollar
GDP per person ($): 8,700
Principal language: English

TRINIDAD & TOBAGO

Capital: Port-of-Spain
Area: 1,980 sq. mi.
Population: 1,295,000
Currency: Trinidad & Tobago dollar
GDP per person ($): 3,600
Principal language: English

GRENADA

St. George's

TOBAGO

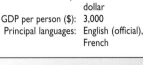

GRENADA

Capital: Saint George's
Area: 133 sq. mi.
Population: 94,486
Currency: East Caribbean dollar
GDP per person ($): 3,000
Principal languages: English (official), French

Port-of-Spain
TRINIDAD

CURAÇAO

Willemstad

Caracas

0		100		200 km

0	50		100 miles

V E N E Z U E L A

A CONTINENT OF CONTRASTS

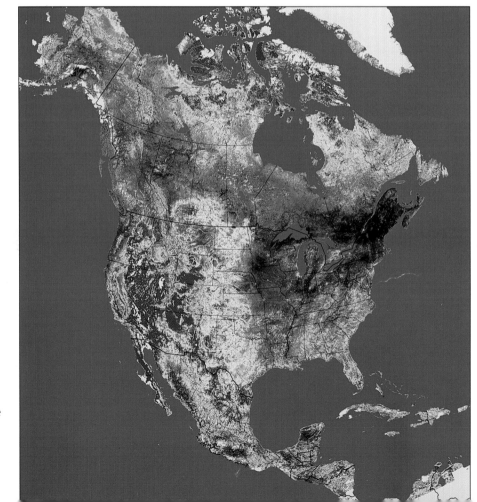

A CONTINENT OF IMMIGRANTS

All North Americans are the descendants of immigrants, even the Native Americans whose ancestors first crossed an ice bridge from northern Asia thousands of years ago. But today the movement of people between countries is not so easy. Large numbers of immigrants entering a country can mean that suddenly there aren't enough resources to go around. Health care, education, and job availability all suffer. Because of this, most wealthy countries try to limit the number of immigrants to arrive. The United States and Canada are particularly careful not to let in so many people that the standard of living drops.

Life in North America blends together contributions from all the peoples who have settled there. In almost any of the continent's great cities you can encounter African cooking, clothes from Europe, the remnants of Native American place names, and Asian architectural styles. All these cultures and many others come together in North America.

Today, North America attracts the attention of people from all over the world. It is a continent of incredible contrasts, containing some of the wealthiest and poorest people on the face of the earth. Contrasts between wealth and poverty become more extreme the farther south you travel. North America can be divided into two types of region.

The continent of North America from space. Superimposed on the photo are the boundaries of different states and countries.

Migrant farmworkers from Mexico clean and pack eggplants on a farm in Texas. Farms in the southern United States rely on the cheap labor Mexican immigrants provide, and Mexicans can earn much more than they would in Mexico.

THE POWERFUL HEARTLAND

At the heart of North America lies the United States, the most powerful country in the world, which dominates the life of the continent. The U.S. economy is the largest in the world, and the United States gives international political leadership to most of the world's countries.

The United States's neighbors are all affected by their closeness to this great country. Most Canadian and Mexican industry is located close to the border with the United States, and these border areas are where many people live. Canada, Mexico, and the United States together are the industrialized heartland of North America. The United States is the most powerful, then Canada and Mexico.

THE FRINGES OF NORTH AMERICA

Away from the heartland of the continent are regions where life is different. In the far north of Canada and Alaska the weather is freezing for much of the year, and almost the only people living in the region are the Native Americans who have been there for hundreds of years. Many people in the far north have lower standards of living than those living in the central band of the continent.

South of Mexico's border with the United States, the warm temperatures make it difficult to move about in the heat of the day. Life goes at a slower pace. There are few truly wealthy people, and many more who have little or nothing. The countries that make up this area of the Caribbean and Central America have varying standards of living, but they are all poor by U.S. or Canadian standards.

**"To my parents the United States was paradise. They were migrant workers, the children of migrant workers. They had never lived in a house. Now they have a really nice home near Nogales, Arizona, with a swimming pool. For many Mexicans the lure of the United States is irresistible. Why wouldn't they risk their lives? You have no idea of the poverty, the filth, the ignorance, and the despair these people have left behind. Being able to stay can mean work that pays well, a clean home, and the end of hunger. It can also mean education for the children and a bright future."
— Jaime Gutierrez, U.S. citizen and son of illegal immigrants**

THE PHYSICAL GEOGRAPHY OF NORTH AMERICA

North America is believed to have once formed part of Pangaea, the gigantic ancient landmass that broke apart to form the continents as we know them today. Over time, the seven continents were formed from this great mass, and they slowly drifted into their respective places on the earth's surface.

The continents are the top parts of massive "plates," which move slowly and press against each other. Much of the physical makeup of eastern North America and western Europe is similar, suggesting that millions of years ago their plates were joined. Eventually the Atlantic Ocean filled the space in between.

Today, the landscape of North America continues to show the movement of the earth's giant plates. As they shift and grind, these plates can cause earthquakes on the United States's west coast, volcanic eruptions in the Caribbean and Central America, or in the past caused the birth of mountain chains such as the Rockies.

Above *Skating on the frozen Rideau Canal in the city of Ottawa, Canada. Winter temperatures in Canada often fall well below freezing, especially in the interior of this vast country.*

Left *In the warmer, southern United States, buildings are designed to keep out the heat. This pueblo, or communal dwelling, in Taos, New Mexico, was built more than 800 years ago by Native Americans. They used adobe mud bricks and built small windows to keep their homes cool.*

CLIMATE

The climate of coastal North America is greatly influenced by the seas that surround the continent. In the east, the Gulf Stream, a current that flows up the east coast from the warm Gulf of Mexico, brings mild winters to the coastal regions. On the west coast, the Pacific Ocean brings warm winters to the continent's edge. Even northern Alaska has ice-free shores during the coldest parts of the winter.

The Gulf of Mexico and the Caribbean are really "arms" of the Atlantic Ocean. Lands in both areas experience generally fair weather, although during warm months tropical air becomes unstable and severe storms can take place. In fact, the months from July through October are generally known as the hurricane season.

As in any continent as vast as North America, the land and climate between the Atlantic and Pacific coasts are wildly variable. Because so much of Canada lies near the extreme northern part of the world, winters are generally bitterly cold, even in the southern provinces. The average January temperature is 0° F. But as you travel south in the continent toward the Tropic of Cancer, the climate becomes more temperate. In the southwestern center of the continent—Arizona, New Mexico, and parts of northern Mexico—the land is desertlike. Finally, in southern Mexico, Central America, and the West Indies, where the sea's influence is strong, the weather is always warm and sometimes wet.

tundra

cooler humid

warmer humid

steppe

desert

savanna

rain forest

The climate to the west can be very wet: the Pacific Northwest gets around 80 inches of rainfall per year.

THE GREAT LAKES AND ST. LAWRENCE

The Great Lakes are five enormous bodies of water that are part of the natural boundary between the United States and Canada. The Great Lakes, along with the St. Lawrence River, form part of the border between the two countries. Together, the five lakes cover 95,000 sq. mi. and form a vast inland freshwater sea. Only one of the Great Lakes, Lake Michigan, lies completely within the United States.

The combination of waterways allows ships to travel 2,300 mi. from the eastern end of Canada more than halfway across the continent. In the 1950s the St. Lawrence River was fitted with a series of locks named the St. Lawrence Seaway, to make navigation easier. In this way large ships could move with greater speed from the Atlantic coast of Canada into the Great Lakes. The seaway also allows travel farther into the winter months, when the river is often frozen over. This water system has helped the growth of commerce and settlement in south-central Canada.

MOUNTAINS

North America includes almost every kind of geographical feature: high, snow-capped mountains, rolling hills and plains, plateaus, swamps, deserts, glaciers, ice fields, volcanoes, and temperate and tropical rain forests.

The Great Western Cordillera mountain chain, which runs from Alaska down the west coast, through Mexico and Central America, is the continent's biggest physical feature. One part of this is the Rocky Mountains, which run north to south through the western third of the continent. These mountains form the Continental Divide: east of the Divide, most rivers drain into the Gulf of Mexico. To the west they empty into the Pacific Ocean.

Parts of North America's east coast are also rocky and hilly. None of the mountains are particularly high compared with the Rockies. This was the first part of the continent to be found by European adventurers. Here they established settlements that still exist today.

The main physical features of North America

GREENLAND

The Norseman Eric the Red discovered and colonized Greenland around A.D. 982. In order to make the barren place appealing to would-be colonists, he gave it the name "Green" land. In fact, the habitable areas form a narrow fringe along the coastline. The center of the vast island is covered by a thick layer of ice remaining from the last ice age. Even in summer, temperatures do not rise much above freezing.

Lying between the North Atlantic and the Arctic Ocean, Greenland is the world's largest island. Much of the region lies within the Arctic Circle. The Arctic Islands to the west of Greenland belong to Canada, whereas Greenland itself is part of Denmark.

The correct name for Greenland is Kalaallit Nunaat. This is the name given to the island country by its native people, the Inuit. Geologically, Greenland is part of the Canadian Shield, which means it is part of the same geologic plate as much of North America.

VOLCANOES

Volcanoes dot many places in the western part of the continent. Oregon is home to Mount St. Helens, a volcano that erupted in 1980, with serious damage and loss of life. Just south of Mexico City, through the large center of the country, chains of mostly extinct volcanoes run east to west across Mexico. This area is known as the volcanic heartland, and it has a dense population. Most of Mexico's farming and industry take place in this region. At 18,700 ft., the country's highest mountain, Pico de Orizaba, is located there.

Many of the islands of the Greater Antilles (including Jamaica, Hispaniola, Cuba, and Puerto Rico) are remains of now-dead volcanic mountaintops that rise from the bottom of the Caribbean. On some islands there are active volcanoes. One of the most famous, Mount Pelee on the island of Martinique, erupted in 1902, killing 28,000 people.

Much of Central America is made up of volcanic mountains, especially along the Pacific coast. In Honduras, for example, volcanoes dot the mountainous area. Irazu erupted in 1963–64, and in 1968 Arenal caused considerable damage. Volcanoes and volcanic ranges have been one of the problems confronting El Salvador over the years. In the south of Guatemala volcanoes have plagued the country for a long time. These volcanoes run along much of Central America's Pacific coast.

Below *Belongings are passed from a boat on the island of St. Thomas, in the U.S. Virgin Islands, after hurricane Marilyn threw it almost 100 ft. from the marina into the street in September 1995. Hurricane season is from July to October in the Caribbean.*

EARTHQUAKES

Where there are volcanoes and volcanic activity, there are often earthquakes. Earthquakes in the region of Mexico City are quite common, and a particularly bad one in 1985 caused about 8,000 deaths and millions of dollars in damage.

A great deal of California lies on or near the San Andreas Fault, a deep crack in the earth's crust that runs north to south for hundreds of miles. The rock on either side of the fault shifts periodically; this means that the area is subject to earthquakes. Many Californians live in fear of large-scale earthquakes, and not without reason. In 1906 and again in 1989 the city of San Francisco was hit by serious earthquakes. In 1994 parts of the Los Angeles area suffered heavy damage and scores of people were killed by a major earthquake that measured 6.8 on the Richter scale.

DESERTS

Not far from Los Angeles is some of the most arid desert in the continent. The hottest and lowest point in the United States is Death Valley in California. A record 132.8° F was recorded there in 1913; the floor of the desert itself is 282 feet below sea level. Deserts occur at the extreme southern and western edges of the Rockies, primarily in the states of Utah, Nevada, and Arizona.

Mexico's northern region consists of Baja California Norte and the states of Sonora, Chihuahua, and Coahuila. This part of the country is mostly desert, and farming is possible only where there are irrigation systems. The extreme west coast of Baja California is desert, although the east coast is largely mountainous. Temperatures vary from 32° F in the winter to a baking 104° F in the summer months.

A scene of devastation in the city of San Francisco after the earthquake of 1989. New buildings in the city are designed and built to be earthquake-proof, but little can be guaranteed in serious earthquakes.

RAIN FORESTS

Mexico's eastern coastal plain, around Tampico, is especially hot and humid with rain forest paralleling the Gulf coast. This area may receive as much as 200 inches of rainfall annually. Large parts of Central America are also covered by rain forest, particularly on the east coast.

Most of the islands of the West Indies were once covered completely with rain forest, but much of this was cleared after the arrival of European settlers, to make way for crops such as sugar and tobacco to be grown.

In the temperate northwest, from Canada down into the northern United States, lies the continent's only temperate rain forest, an expanse of Douglas fir, Sitka spruce, and Pacific red cedar.

Above *Tropical rain forest on the island of St. Lucia, in the Caribbean*
Below *The Gateway Arch rises alongside the Mississippi at St. Louis, Missouri.*

THE PRAIRIES

In the center of North America, stretching from Saskatchewan to Oklahoma and from Wyoming to Illinois, are the prairies. These grasslands are today used almost entirely for farming, especially for growing wheat and corn. They are long, flat landscapes, sometimes with low hills breaking up the horizon.

THE MISSISSIPPI

The Mississippi, one of the world's longest rivers, starts as a trickle in northern Minnesota near the Canadian border and runs south, dividing the United States roughly in half. It empties into the Gulf of Mexico at New Orleans. Along the way the Missouri and Ohio rivers flow into the Mississippi. Together they form the longest river system on the continent, at 3,709 miles.

DISCOVERY AND EXPLORATION

BEFORE THE EUROPEANS

Before the 15th century, when European nations turned their interests westward, only the Indians lived on the North American continent. The people were blissfully unaware that their existence was about to be threatened and changed forever.

When the Spanish arrived in Mexico in 1519 they found an already flourishing civilization, that of the Aztecs. And before the Aztecs, there had been an even more highly developed civilization—the Mayan—which dated to about the first century A.D. The Maya were skilled farmers who also studied stars and invented a very accurate calendar. They seem to have been the first North Americans to develop a system of writing, using pictures, much like that of the ancient Egyptians. The Maya built impressive stepped pyramids of stone and other large structures that they covered with elaborate carvings. The Maya were conquered by a later group, the Toltecs. The Toltecs in turn were conquered by the warlike Aztecs.

Farther to the north, Indian groups developed ways of life that allowed them to exist in the varied environments of North America, from the Pueblo peoples of the desert southwest to the Innu and Cree of the subarctic regions.

The Pyramid of the Sun, on the Teotihuacan archaeological site in Mexico, where the Aztecs worshiped. The Aztecs controlled most of central Mexico from the 15th century until the Spanish conquistador Hernan Cortes arrived, in 1519.

EUROPEAN EXPLORERS

Norsemen from Scandinavia, the Vikings, were probably the first European navigators to visit North America, but their settlements were few and quickly disappeared.

When the Italian Christopher Columbus sailed westward from Spain in 1492, he and his sailors were looking for a shorter route to India. But Columbus's ships landed at Watling Island in the Bahamas: he had stumbled across two unknown continents (North and South America) and the "New World" was born. Because Columbus thought he had reached part of India, he called the islands the Indies and the natives he found living there Indians. The Spanish soon established settlements in the Americas, and made the native peoples into slaves for their mines and farms.

THE CONQUEST OF MEXICO

Hernan Cortes landed near Veracruz in 1519. The Aztecs were in power when the Spanish began their conquest of Mexico in that same year. Cortes appointed himself the ruler of Mexico and first imprisoned and then executed Montezuma, the Aztec king. Cortes took land from the natives and made them work as slaves.

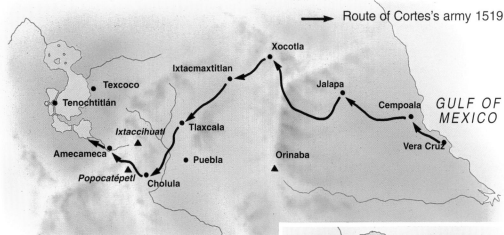

Route of Cortes's army 1519

The Spanish brought European diseases with them. Smallpox, influenza, measles, chicken pox, and typhus were illnesses against which the Aztecs had no resistance. During the conquest of Mexico there was an outbreak of smallpox that killed thousands. Aztecs who were not killed by diseases were worked to death in silver and gold mines and on sugar plantations by the Spanish.

By 1521, the Spanish conquest of Mexico by Hernan Cortes and his conquistadors was complete. There were roughly 10 million Aztecs living in what is now Mexico when Cortes arrived. By the time the conquest of Mexico was over, there were only about a million Aztecs left in the whole empire. Spain had control of Mexico and much of Central America for almost 300 years.

VOLCANOES AND TURKEYS

When the Spanish first arrived in the Americas, they were astonished by volcanoes. They had never seen anything like them in Europe. In the New World the Spanish also became acquainted with new products: they found corn, sweet potatoes, tomatoes, peanuts, turkeys, chocolate, potatoes, tobacco, and rubber. The Spaniards themselves brought, among other things, horses, cattle, sheep, goats, donkeys, wheat, sugarcane, pigs, and chickens.

Right A mural showing life in Mexico in the early days of the Spanish conquest. Aztec slaves can be seen at work in the background.

THE ENGLISH, FRENCH, AND DUTCH ARRIVE

The English were not far behind the Spanish. John Cabot, an Italian-born explorer sailing under the English flag, discovered the eastern part of Canada in 1497. He was followed in 1534 by the French explorer Jacques Cartier, who planted a cross on the Gaspé Peninsula, on mainland Canada's east coast.

The first permanent English settlement was established in 1607 at Jamestown, Virginia. The settlers were colonists, wanting only the chance to claim new land—and a new and different life. Virginia's early capital, Williamsburg, has been restored and is maintained as a living museum, where visitors can experience a working colonial settlement that is still very much as it was in the seventeenth and eighteenth centuries.

THE BIRTH OF CANADA

Four wars, fought between Great Britain and France from 1689 to 1760 over territory in the New World, were known as the French and Indian Wars. In 1763 the British ended these wars and wrested all of Canada from the French. Even today Canada remains a confederation with strong ties to the British government.

Above A drawing of the Pilgrim Fathers arriving at Plymouth, Massachusetts, in 1620. The pilgrims were a group of English who sailed to America on a boat named the Mayflower, to escape religious persecution back home.

Right An engraving showing the battle of Quebec in 1759, one of many battles fought between the French and the British over the control of Canada. British troops are shown scrambling up a woody bank, to fire on French troops at the top.

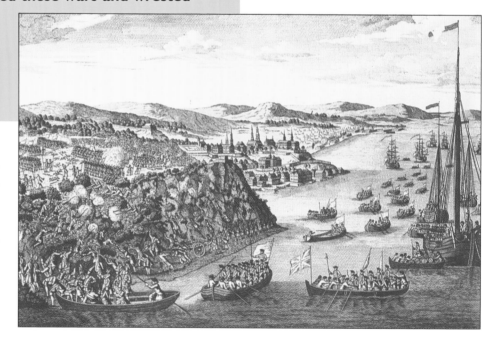

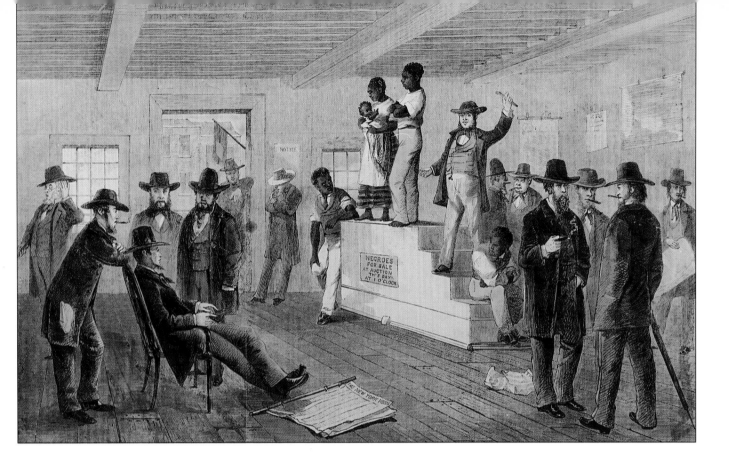

SLAVERY

Throughout the early years of European expansion into North America, people from Africa were brought to the continent as slaves. The Europeans had first forced Indians into working for them, but so many died that more slaves were needed. A triangular trade grew, with ships taking trade goods from Europe to Africa, slaves from Africa to the Americas, and sugar, rum, and tobacco from the Americas back to Europe.

During the eighteenth and nineteenth centuries the triangular trade died out, because more and more countries banned trading in slaves. In the United States, slavery was ended only after a terrible civil war (1861–65) between northern and southern states. In the Caribbean, the whole economy was based on slave labor, but the practice died out in the 19th century as the colonial powers banned it one by one.

By the beginning of the 20th century, the descendants of these earliest settlers were living across North America: in the English-speaking lands of the United States and Canada (which also includes French speakers); in the lands of Mexico and Central America, where Spanish is the official language; and in the Caribbean.

A drawing of a slave auction in 1861, the same year that the Civil War broke out over the issue of slavery. Southern states fought to keep slavery because slave labor was so important to the economy of their huge plantations. Northern states argued that it was barbaric to allow the practice to continue.

RELIGIOUS REFUGEES

Many emigrants came to North America for freedom to practice their religions:

- **The Pilgrims founded the Massachusetts Bay Colony in 1620. Their religious beliefs had been threatened in England, and they left their homes to seek religious freedom.**

- **In 1628 the Puritans, an extremist sect of the Church of England, arrived.**

- **In 1634, Roman Catholics fled persecution in England and established what is now the state of Maryland.**

THE PEOPLE AND THEIR CULTURES

When European settlers came to the New World they had a unique chance to create a new society. True, there would be many elements of the old way of life, but it would still be a land where settlers and their descendants could experiment with the new.

In many ways the first settlers were successful—North America is a continent like no other, where ideals of liberty and equality before the law are meaningful for most of the population. Like most other industrialized nations, North America has problems—the most serious is the gap between its rich and poor. But today, life in North America combines influences from Europe, from Africa, and—more recently—from Asia, which have mixed with many Native American cultural elements.

Vancouver is one of Canada's industrial cities on the Pacific coast, where the culture reflects its immigrants.

THE COLD NORTHLANDS

The farthest northern regions of North America are very sparsely populated, especially in Canada and Alaska. Canada's Northwest Territories and Yukon Territory are underpopulated. Some 52 percent of the people are Indians. The land is valuable mainly for hunting and forestry except in the northernmost area where it is too cold for trees to grow. Almost the only other industries are mineral extraction and defense—Canada and the United States built a series of listening posts in the far north, during the Cold War (1950–89). Their job was to guard against attacks from the Soviet Union.

Almost 27,000 Inuit people live in the Northwest Territories, in the extreme northernmost part of Canada. In 1993 the Canadian government turned part of the Northwest Territories into the Nunavut Territory. This will give the Inuit there a greater voice in how they are governed.

In Alaska, the northernmost of the United States, the situation is slightly different because of the state's oil reserves. Oil has brought work and some prosperity to Alaska, but the region is still thinly populated and underdeveloped. Much of the wealth from oil has gone to large towns such as Anchorage and Valdez, both ports on the south coast from which oil is shipped. Many of the native peoples of Alaska still live in comparative poverty in isolated rural settlements.

In one way, though, the wealth from oil benefits all Alaskans. Every year the state pays a dividend to all U.S. citizens resident in Alaska. The money comes from payments made by the oil companies to the state goverment.

Indigenous women in the Arctic north of Canada's Northwest Territories, outside their home.

⌐E CENTRAL STRIP

⌐the central strip of North ⌐America—from Canada's industrialized zone heading southward—the culture of European immigrants dominates. Most people speak English, which is also the language of government in Canada and the United States. The standard of living is high in southern Canada and in the United States for those people who have jobs and work hard. The bulk of the population lives in the many large cities that are sprinkled across this region of North America.

The great city of New York still influences what happens throughout the United States. Despite competition from other large U.S. cities, it is the financial, commercial, and artistic center of the country. Every day more than seven million residents work there and enjoy the cultural and artistic events that New York City offers. For many immigrants to the United States, the Statue of Liberty, on an island near the entrance to New York Harbor, has provided a welcoming sight since 1886.

Three of the U.S.'s largest cities—Dallas, Houston, and San Antonio—are in Texas. To the east is Louisiana, a state whose settlement by the French in the seventeenth century has always given the area a French-American character. The city of New Orleans, at the delta where the Mississippi empties into the Gulf of Mexico, has long remained a popular tourist attraction for its blend of jazz, southern architecture, and fine restaurants that serve the famous and popular Cajun cuisine. Other great cities include Los Angeles, home to the U.S. movie industry; Seattle, center of the aircraft industry; and Detroit, site of most U.S. car manufacturing. Detroit shows clearly the United States's relationship with Canada. Right on the border, Detroit's sister city in Canada is Windsor, Ontario. The motor industry made both cities prosperous, and its decline has hit both of them hard.

New York City's famous Wall Street is the financial center of both the city and the nation. Business in the stock exchange and banks of Wall Street affects the economy of the world.

SOUTH OF THE BORDER

Although the northern border zone of Mexico is now heavily industrialized, the rest of Central America is less well developed. Farther from the border, life gets harder and harder. In many ways Mexico is still a very poor country, and there is a wide gulf between rich and poor. Most of the division lies between the urban and rural populations, with more and more people coming into cities to seek better paying jobs and more interesting careers. As a result, many overcrowded cities have vast slums—packed, dirty urban areas lacking decent hygienic conditions and basic services.

Some 60 percent of Mexicans are mestizos, people of mixed European and Indian descent. Most of the rest are Indian or Hispanic. Almost 95 percent of the population speaks Spanish.

The western coastal plain is one of the poorest regions in Mexico, and the permanent population is small. The famous Pacific coast resort of Acapulco draws visitors who seek sun and surf. The Yucatán Peninsula brings as many as three million visitors a year. Tourism has also profited by the development of Cancún, a popular Yucatán resort. Even the seasonal hurricanes that often plague this region do little to deter visitors. Yucatán is also the site of spectacular Mayan ruins, including Chichén Itzá.

Below Mexico City lies high up on the central plateau on the site of the ancient Aztec capital of Tenochtitlán. This ancient city, built around A.D. 1325, was originally constructed by the Aztecs on a network of artificial islands in the middle of Lake Texcoco.

MEXICO CITY

Mexico City is a thriving, modern business center with branches of most multinational corporations. The center of the city boasts many buildings dating to the early Spanish colonial period side by side with modern skyscrapers. The city has grown rapidly over the last 20 years, and by some statistics is regarded as the largest city in the world.

At an altitude of 7,800 ft., Mexico City is high enough to cause breathing problems for people not used to such altitude. In the 1968 Olympics, many athletes had difficulties adjusting to the reduced oxygen level in Mexico City.

Left Homes like this one are common in the shantytowns of Mexico City. The city cannot cope with the number of people arriving from the countryside looking for work.

CENTRAL AMERICA AND THE CARIBBEAN

Along the Caribbean coast of Central America and on the Caribbean islands themselves, the population is largely of mixed Afro-American and Indian descent. The inaccessible interior of Central America is home to Indians who are pure blooded and maintain much of the way of life of their Mayan ancestors.

Many Caribbean people are descendants of Africans brought to the West Indies to work as slaves. Black Africans fought hard against the way they were treated. Slave rebellions were common and reached their greatest achievement in 1804. In Haiti the former slave Toussaint L'Ouverture led a rebellion that resulted in Haiti's becoming an independent country where slavery was banned.

The Caribbean islands have had a unique effect on popular culture, particularly with their music. Reggae, ska, calypso, soca, and other musical styles all first appeared in the Caribbean. The limbo became a favorite party dance in the 1960s.

PUERTO RICO

Puerto Rico's large population (about 3.8 million people) is almost all Spanish-speaking, although officially English and Spanish are equal languages. Puerto Rico is now a commonwealth and self-governing part of the United States. Almost 2.7 million additional Puerto Ricans live on the mainland of the United States, mostly in Florida and in major American cities. Once one of the poorest and most exploited of the Caribbean islands, in the last 50 years a major program of development has been instituted. It has largely been successful, and both manufacturing and tourism have helped with this new step toward prosperity.

A man in carnival costume on the island of Trinidad, in the Caribbean. Carnival was first celebrated in Trinidad when Catholics settled there about 200 years ago. At first only white people were allowed to take part. After slavery was ended in 1833, the festival became the celebration of freedom for black people. Today, carnival is a major festival in the Caribbean, with calypso songs and costumed parades in the streets.

Religion in Central America and the Caribbean is often a mixture of the Roman Catholicism of the Spanish, Indian beliefs, and the religions of West Africa brought by slaves. One of the most famous examples is voodoo, which is a popular religion in Haiti. One of the many features of voodoo is the belief in zombies. Zombies are dead humans who have been reanimated to serve as slaves to evil voodoo priests. Similar religions include santeria and candomble.

Above Fruit and vegetables are sold by small-scale farmers at a traditional roadside market in Belize City.

On almost all the islands of the Caribbean, tourism has become the main source of income in the late 20th century. The weather is generally perfect, and entertainment, hotels, and food are relatively cheap. Large cruise ships and frequent flights from many points on the globe bring in travelers by the thousands, who are looking for balmy temperatures, clear blue waters, and golden beaches.

Below As Mexico becomes wealthier, people are enjoying modern luxuries in an increasing number of homes.

Education is readily available to most people in the majority of North American countries. On average, literacy rates are high, but in some parts of Central America and the Caribbean, school attendance is very low.

AGRICULTURE AND FISHING

FARMING IN THE CENTRAL BELT

The Great Farms of the Continent

The largest and most significant agricultural areas in North America lie in the center of the continent, in southern Canada and much of the middle of the United States. Manitoba, Saskatchewan, and Alberta form Canada's heartland. The states directly to the south in the United States are geographical continuations of these gently rolling, flat grasslands and prairies. Three-quarters of all farming and cattle grazing takes place in this part of the continent. Some 30 percent of Saskatchewan is covered by fields, and wheat is the main crop on 20 percent of the farms there.

Canadian farms are sizable, averaging 750 acres. Most of the wheat grown in this region is made into flour for home use and for export. On this level land, agricultural machinery speeds the planting, cultivating, and harvesting processes. But rainfall is not always dependable, and much of the land needs irrigation to ensure successful crops. Today, cattle grazing has surpassed crop growing in importance, although 60 percent of Canada's income comes from a combination of these two activities.

The middle region of the United States, with the land on either side of the Mississippi, forms the great central plains of the Midwest, where most of the country's grain products are grown. The area is often known as America's heartland or even America's breadbasket. The weather tends to be temperate, making it ideal for growing crops. As in much of the central United States, winters can be severe and summers very hot.

In the last hundred years farming in the United States and Canada has become a struggle for survival. The U.S. government has provided farmers with financial aid to maintain their agricultural livelihoods. This money helps in the short term, but it doesn't actually mean that farming is profitable.

A combine harvester at work in Iowa, part of a region known as the country's breadbasket, because of the amount of grain that is produced.

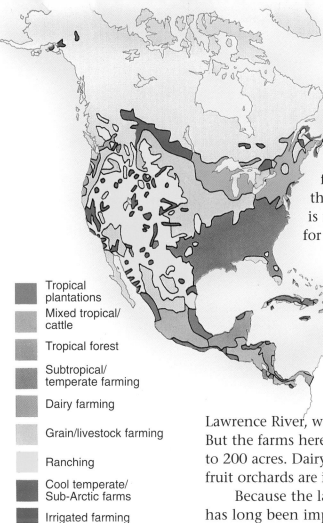

Tropical plantations

Mixed tropical/ cattle

Tropical forest

Subtropical/ temperate farming

Dairy farming

Grain/livestock farming

Ranching

Cool temperate/ Sub-Arctic farms

Irrigated farming

Nonfarming regions

Small-scale Farming

North of the prairie states lie Michigan, Wisconsin, and Minnesota. Winters there can be severe, with temperatures sometimes falling as low as -40° F. But in the summer the dense green pastures provide ideal grazing land for animals, and Wisconsin is sometimes called the Dairy State. Most of the land around the Rockies is mountainous and hilly, although some is suitable for cattle grazing.

Much of the Canadian provinces of Ontario and Quebec is rolling farmland surrounded by woods and lakes. Good, but small-scale, farming is available on the peninsula between Lakes Ontario, Huron, and Erie. The Great Lakes help keep the climate fairly mild, but water from them is sucked up into the atmosphere and during winter can mean heavy snowfalls. In many places bordered by the St. Lawrence River, woods, waterways, and pastureland exist side by side. But the farms here are generally small family holdings, averaging 150 to 200 acres. Dairy farms abound both in Ontario and Quebec, but fruit orchards are important to Ontario's economy.

Because the land is often gentle and rolling, small-scale farming has long been important in the mid-Atlantic states. Farther south is very fertile land, and many years ago large plantations that grew vast amounts of tobacco and cotton were the centers of southern U.S. life. Today the farms of the south still exist, but on a much smaller scale. The weather is warm or hot and often very humid, making for good growing seasons, and the land is rich and green.

FEWER WORKERS, MORE MACHINES

Farming in the central belt of North America has undergone tremendous changes in the last 50 years. One-fifth of Canadians live in rural areas, but only four percent are farmers. And in the United States only two percent of workers are engaged in farming. As the number of individual farms has decreased and the use of machinery instead of manual labor has increased, the actual sizes of the farms have grown.

Right *One person and a machine now do the work that several people used to do more than 50 years ago.*

FARMING IN CENTRAL AMERICA AND THE CARIBBEAN

Farther south in the continent, agriculture is very different. For example, almost half of Mexico is mountainous or arid. The country is not really suitable for farming (although in recent years irrigation systems have aided agriculture). Where it can be grown, the major crop is corn. Where the land is not quite good enough for farming, it is often used for grazing animals. Since most of the Yucatan peninsula is composed of limestone, farming is difficult, but there is some cattle ranching.

Because of the abundant rain farther to the south, fruits, coffee beans, and coconuts grow there. Some farming and cattle grazing are done on the western coastal plain, and there is a wealth of hydroelectric power that helps provide electricity for paper mills.

Only about 6 percent of Central American land is suitable for farming. Even so, crops such as coffee and bananas provide employment for about half the residents. Because these products are exported, they provide Central American and Caribbean countries with valuable foreign income. Bananas are one of Central America's most important crops, and more than half of them are exported.

Although agriculture is still important in Central America and the Caribbean, there is also increasing industrialization. More and more, as in most of North America, service industries such as tourism are becoming an important source of income.

Above *Bananas and vegetables for sale in a roadside market on the island of St. Lucia, in the Caribbean*

Left *Newly picked avocados are sorted on the banks of Lake Atitlan, in Guatemala. Much farming in Central America is still done without the use of machinery.*

FISHING

The vast fishing grounds near the Atlantic Ocean coast first drew explorers to Canada's Maritime Provinces. The famed Grand Banks, south and east of Newfoundland, have always been among the best fishing grounds in the world. Cod and lobsters are among the largest catches there. Even today, fishing is still important to the local residents, although the income from fishing only accounts for about one percent of Canada's total revenue. Canada's lakes and rivers provide some of the best recreational fishing in the world.

Fishing remains a vital industry on the Pacific Northwest coast, with salmon as the number one catch. But today many fish are raised on fish farms, which help produce pollution-free fish.

Mexico and the Central American countries that have Pacific coastlines all have commercial fishing fleets. Anchovies are one important catch, although overfishing has meant that sometimes there aren't enough fish available. Because of this, the fleets have had to allow the fish stocks to recover.

On a much smaller scale, fishing is important to the people who live around the Caribbean Sea and Gulf of Mexico. Restaurants throughout the region, from the Texas coast to Trinidad, all serve a wide choice of fish. People also catch fish to eat for themselves. Fish can be an important source of protein for poorer people.

Above Cod is cleaned in a fishing village in Quebec province, Canada.

Below Nicaragua's largest sugar mill, in the town of Chichigalpa. Nicaragua, like the Dominican Republic, is badly affected when world prices drop for its export crops. The main crops are coffee, sugar, and bananas.

AT THE MERCY OF THE MARKET

There is a downside to being as dependent on a single crop as some Central American/Caribbean nations. A country such as the Dominican Republic, where sugar is the most important crop and export, has suffered recently as the international price of sugar has dropped. In many Central American and Caribbean countries there has been great concern, especially during periods when the price of their main crops tapered off during the worldwide recession of the 1990s.

RESOURCES AND INDUSTRY

RESOURCES

In the northern part of Ontario lies the Canadian Shield. The shield is an area that extends from Lake Superior north to the Arctic Islands and from western Canada eastward to Greenland. It is made up of ancient rock, some of which is between 570 million years and 3 billion years old! A hilly region with plenty of small lakes, the soil is poor. There are rich mineral deposits, especially zinc, nickel, iron ore, and lead. The lowland area south of Hudson Bay has good forests that support a lumber industry. Much of this land is swampy in the summer, but the northern half of the bay is bounded by tundra all year.

Copper is British Columbia's most valuable mineral resource. There are few urban areas in the Northwest Territories, but the name of one of them tells a story: Uranium City has a large supply of one of the world's most important resources. Uranium is used in nuclear reactors and is therefore important today for use in nuclear power stations.

In the United States, Pennsylvania has rich deposits of coal, iron ore, and oil, which are used in the steel-making process. Steel once made Pittsburgh an important industrial center. Today, however, steel can be manufactured more efficiently and cheaply outside North America, so the industry has declined. Now, much of the heavy manufacturing of the nineteenth and early twentieth centuries has given way to service industries such as banking, retailing, and the restaurant business.

There are large deposits of mineral ores in northern Mexico. The silver that the Spanish conquistadors carried off in abundance is still mined, but textiles and handicrafts are also important industries. Central America, though, has few valuable mineral deposits or fuels, so these resources contribute little to the area's national income.

Like Central America, the Caribbean lacks major mineral resources, although there are scattered industries such as bauxite production in Jamaica. Bauxite is a mineral used in the production of aluminum.

Below The Kennecott copper mine in Utah is the largest open-pit mine in the world. It is so big that it can be seen from space.

Above A cement factory sits directly beside a soccer field and housing in Mexico City. The city is home to about half of Mexico's manufacturing industry.

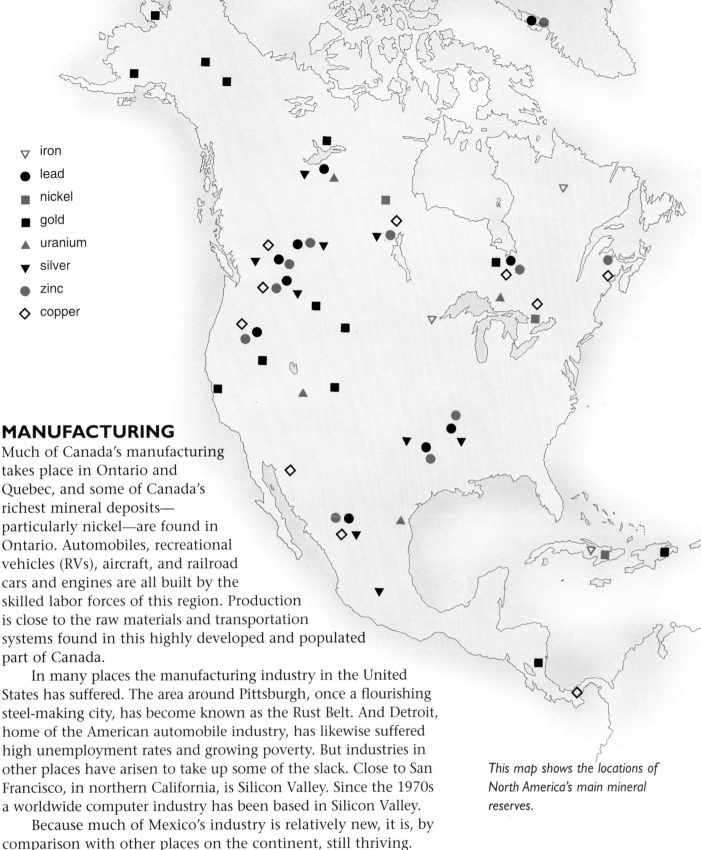

Key

▽ iron
● lead
■ nickel
■ gold
▲ uranium
▼ silver
● zinc
◇ copper

MANUFACTURING

Much of Canada's manufacturing takes place in Ontario and Quebec, and some of Canada's richest mineral deposits—particularly nickel—are found in Ontario. Automobiles, recreational vehicles (RVs), aircraft, and railroad cars and engines are all built by the skilled labor forces of this region. Production is close to the raw materials and transportation systems found in this highly developed and populated part of Canada.

In many places the manufacturing industry in the United States has suffered. The area around Pittsburgh, once a flourishing steel-making city, has become known as the Rust Belt. And Detroit, home of the American automobile industry, has likewise suffered high unemployment rates and growing poverty. But industries in other places have arisen to take up some of the slack. Close to San Francisco, in northern California, is Silicon Valley. Since the 1970s a worldwide computer industry has been based in Silicon Valley.

Because much of Mexico's industry is relatively new, it is, by comparison with other places on the continent, still thriving. Many of Mexico's manufacturing businesses are close to the border with the United States and are owned by U.S. companies. The companies cross the border to Mexico because it is cheaper to produce goods there: factories are cheaper to build or buy, and labor is cheaper. Only small-scale manufacturing is found in much of Central America and the West Indies islands.

This map shows the locations of North America's main mineral reserves.

FORESTRY

Forests abound, but not in the extreme northern regions, where it is too cold for trees to survive. More than one-third of Canada is forested, with some 150 different kinds of trees. In British Columbia, the forests are rich and dense, and the forestry industry is one of the biggest moneymakers in this part of Canada. Canada is one of the world's leading producers of wood pulp and paper.

Along the Pacific coast of North America lie some of the world's best forests. Extremely mild and rainy, Oregon has one of the world's few temperate rain forests. Forests abound in southeast Mexico, Central America, and parts of the Caribbean. Wood—especially mahogany and cedar—is a major export.

FOREST GIANTS

Just north of California's San Francisco Bay area are found the giant sequoia, or redwood, trees. Some of these ancient trees are so large that arches have been carved in their trunks and cars are able to drive through. The largest redwood, named General Sherman, is believed to weigh 1,400 tons. Not far away are gentle, sunny hillsides, where some of the country's finest grapes are grown, and wines that are sold the world over are produced.

OIL

Oil has brought wealth to several parts of North America. Texas's growth and prosperity were largely due to the discovery of oil in 1901. Oil was discovered in Calgary, Alberta, in 1947, and the province found a new prosperity. There are also oil rigs in the Gulf of Mexico and off the coast of California.

In the last 50 years, Mexico's single most important export has become oil. In the Yucatán, there are large natural gas and oil fields. Because Mexico has become highly industrialized, much of this raw material is refined and used locally.

Work on a Mexican oil refinery. Mexico is one of the world's largest exporters of oil, most of which is drilled offshore in the Gulf of Mexico.

Above *Silicon Valley is an area south of San Francisco. It is the center of the U.S. computer industry.*

SERVICE INDUSTRIES

In the last 20 years, service industries have grown in much of North America. Service industries provide services, rather than products, to people. These may include banking, restaurants, entertainment, and tourism.

Tourism is a growth industry in much of North America. Visitors to Canada from the United States like the fact that their northern neighbors speak the same language. The nearby country is a lot like home and provides interesting cities and vast wildernesses to explore.

For most of the islands in the Caribbean, the biggest industry is tourism and the service industries associated with it. Visitors come to enjoy the beaches and warm seas, but there are also clubs, restaurants, casinos, beach activities such as windsurfing, and sightseeing tours.

FUR TRAPPING

Because of Canada's generally sparse population, there are still many animals in the country's forests. As a result, the supply of animal furs has always been a source of wealth in this region. Only Russia and Canada count trapping animals for fur as major industries, largely because of their northerly positions, relatively sparse population, and the tremendous size of their forests. Animals are hunted in the winter, when their furs are thickest. Today many Natives and Inuit still trap animals for their skins, to use for themselves and to sell for cash.

Right *In northern Quebec, Canada, a caribou skin is stretched on a frame to be cleaned and dried.*

POLITICS AND POLITICAL SYSTEMS

As they became independent in the eighteenth and nineteenth centuries, most North American countries rejected the idea of monarchy and decided to set up democratic governments. The emphasis was to be on government by the people's representatives. To a large extent this has been carried out.

Canada is made up of ten provinces, with Ottawa as the capital. National decisions are made by the prime minister and his or her cabinet, supported by a parliament. Each of Canada's provinces also has its own regional government.

American citizens vote for a president every four years, usually from one of the two major political parties: Democrats and Republicans. Each state is represented in the two-part Congress: the two parts are the Senate and the House of Representatives. As well as Congress, there are the Judicial Branch of the government (which sits in judgment on the laws), and the Executive Branch, headed by the president. No one branch can take control of another. Each state also has its own regional government.

Above American president Bill Clinton (center), who was elected in November 1992 and reelected in 1996.

WASHINGTON, D.C.

Washington (District of Columbia) was designed with broad avenues and wide open spaces. Named for George Washington, the first president, it has been the nation's capital since 1800. Since then, all presidents have worked and lived in the White House. The Capitol, about a mile away, holds both houses of Congress: the Senate and the House of Representatives. This is where the nation's laws are proposed, debated, and passed. Nearby is the Supreme Court building, where the country's laws are upheld and interpreted.

Below Landmarks of Washington, D.C.: from left to right, the Lincoln Memorial, the Washington Monument, and the Capitol.

Mexico is a republic, with a constitution that was established in 1917. An elected president is the head of state. Laws are made by two bodies: the Senate and the Chamber of Deputies. The Revolutionary Party has been in control ever since 1929. Prior to that, a repressive government under the dictatorship of Porfirio Diaz lasted from 1876 to 1911. He began the trend of letting the rich get richer and keeping the poor without any power, a policy that has, with some exceptions, lasted to the present.

Except for Belize, which is still administered by Great Britain, all the countries of Central America are republics. This means that, in theory, the governments are led by representatives elected by the people. Great Britain's last colony in North America, Belize achieved independence in 1981, although it is a parliamentary democracy whose head of state is the British monarch.

Costa Rica gained its independence from Spain in 1821, and in the late 19th century orderly government was set up. By 1949 a democratic constitution was in place and, with only minor difficulties over the years, Costa Rica has been a successful country with a well-educated population.

Some Central American countries have made the transition to independence easily; others have not. Although Guatemala has been a republic since 1839, the country has had a long history of unstable governments. In the 20th century, Guatemala has often been under military rule, and there have been many violations of human rights.

Mexico's former president, Carlos Salinas de Gortiari, who was in office from 1987–94. Stories surround Salinas and his alleged involvement in the murder of another political figure, Francisco Ruiz Massieu.

In the 1980s, the United States contributed to Nicaragua's upheavals by campaigning against the Sandinista government, which was backed by the communist-led governments of the then-USSR and Cuba. The United States endorsed the Contra rebels, supplying them with guns and resources. In 1990, U.S.-supported Violeta de Chamorro was elected president by a population worn out by the effects of U.S. actions that also included economic sanctions.

THE PANAMA CANAL

In the late 19th century, the United States investigated the possibility of building a canal through Nicaragua. The canal would eliminate sailing around all of South America to get from the east to the west coast of North America. Eventually the U.S. built that canal across a narrow strip of land in the country to the south, Panama. In 1914, the first ships passed through the 50.6-mile-long canal. It was a triumph of engineering cut through rain forest and malaria-ridden swamps as well as hills of solid rock. The canal cut 8,000 mi., weeks of sailing time, and untold millions of dollars from the journey.

Panama was once part of Colombia, and in 1903 the country was given its independence with U.S. support. The United States saw Panama's value primarily as the site for the now-famous Panama Canal, which was begun in 1900. A thin strip of land within Panama became the Panama Canal Zone, under American administration. This land will be returned to Panama in 2000.

A cruise ship enters a system of locks on the Panama Canal.

The United States has campaigned in a similar way to overthrow the communist government of Cuba. Cuba is one of the largest and most important of the Caribbean islands. The western end of the island is only 90 mi. from Key West, at the southernmost tip of Florida. Since 1959, Cuba has been led by the communist government of Fidel Castro, who overthrew the corrupt leader Batista. Despite economic and sometimes military pressure from the United States, Cuba has high literacy and employment rates and one of the best health care records in North America.

Left *Fidel Castro (center), Cuba's leader and head of the communist government, at the opening of a special school. Castro has been Cuba's leader since 1959. The United States would like him and his government replaced.*

In recent times Haiti has been the site of political unrest, largely stemming from the 28-year-long dictatorship of the notorious Duvalier family. Following the 1986 ousting of the last Duvalier, Jean Aristide came to power. But unrest and struggle continued, and Aristide was forced to resign in 1991. The United States then imposed strong embargos on Haitian goods, and the economy suffered. At the time, some 35,000 Haitians, poorly equipped with inadequate boats, tried to sail to the United States, where they were denied entry. The situation improved somewhat when Aristide was restored to power in 1994. In the meantime Haiti became a land stripped bare of its trees. Parts of it are now little more than desert, and the future for most Haitians is grim.

"My brother Reginald and I both work for the same large U.S. corporation. We came to the United States because, frankly, this is still the land of opportunity. Even though we both had good scientific educations, there were just no chances for us in Haiti. Anyone who is talented or educated wants to get out—and almost always for the U.S.

"We still have family there and we like the island way of life. If our jobs for an American multinational sent us there, we might consider going back, but we'd miss the American health care facilities and the general standard of living."
—Maxime Pleiade, engineer in the United States, native of Haiti

Right The Haitian president Jean Aristide (center), at the Pentagon in Washington, D.C. in September 1994, before he was restored to power.

BORDERS AND WHAT THEY MEAN

A border control policeman on the Mexico-U.S. border arrests a Mexican trying to cross the border illegally.

ILLEGAL IMMIGRATION

The industrialized area of North America attracts immigrants from other parts of the continent. This is particularly true of the United States. Some immigrants enter the United States legally, but many come to the country uninvited.

There are nine Border Patrol sectors along the Mexico-U.S. border. As many as one million people trying to enter the United States illegally across this border are caught by U.S. border guards each year. No one is sure how many illegal immigrants, who come from Mexico and other Central American countries, get through.

Some figures indicate that, of the two million agricultural workers in the United States, as many as 70 percent are Mexican. The bulk of these are illegal immigrants.

DRUGS

A newer issue that plagues the Mexico-U.S. border is that of drug smuggling. In recent years, cocaine, marijuana, and heroin have been transported into the United States, and officials are aware that substantial amounts of the substances have come across the Mexican border. Most of the drugs originate in South America, but Mexico is a staging point for drugs heading into the United States. Today, trained drug-sniffing dogs and special X-ray devices are in place to keep this problem to a minimum, although still only a small percentage of drug traffickers are detected, caught, and arrested.

Many Central American countries are major sources for illegal drugs entering the United States. U.S. intervention in Central American affairs has been viewed as outside interference. But the United States sees controlling the traffic in arms and drugs in Central America as essential to its national security. The densely forested mountain regions hide farms where drugs are grown in small, cleared areas. Or they conceal secret laboratories where drugs are refined and manufactured. Networks of drug lords, bribed government officials, and corrupt law enforcement officers all contribute to an atmosphere of organized crime. While poor people can make themselves rich through the drug trade, there is little hope that the steady flow of illegal narcotics will stop.

Above *In May 1995, Jose Sosa Mayorga was arrested on suspicion of drug trafficking. He is thought to hold an important position in a large Mexican drug-trafficking organization.*

NAFTA

In 1994 a major agreement went into effect concerning trade between the United States, Canada, and Mexico. This is the North American Free Trade Agreement, usually called NAFTA. The treaty's intent was to lower tariffs on the exchange of goods between these three countries and to make trading among them more open and easy.

Just two years after the agreement went into effect, U.S. corporations seemed to be the big winners from the agreement. Production costs are lower outside the industrialized central band, but the finished products are still sold in the United States at regular prices. Hundreds of thousands of U.S. workers have lost their manufacturing jobs as factories have moved south of the border.

WHY EMIGRATE?

Even with the vigorous social, educational, economic, and industrial reform programs undertaken at various points in the 20th century, the standard of living for the majority of the Mexican population lags far behind that of Canada and the United States. For this reason, emigration to the U.S. has always been an attractive alternative. One man, recently detained at a border crossing, was certain he could earn $12,000 a year in the United States as opposed to the $1,500 he had earned by doing odd jobs in Mexico.

Left *The difference in the quality of life available in the United States, compared with that in some Central American countries, means that emigration to the United States is still the dream of millions.*

THE FUTURE OF NORTH AMERICA

POLLUTION

Common to almost all the countries of North America are environmental issues that need to be addressed for the benefit of future generations. The industrialization of the central strip has not come without an environmental cost: pollution of rivers and lakes; the disruption of underground aquifers; soil depleted of all its nutrients, and dumps of toxic chemicals are all part of the North American environment. Although the industrialized countries—Canada, the United States, and Mexico—bear the largest responsibility, every country needs to consider how to safeguard the air, water, and soil. The issue of acid rain is especially critical in the United States and Canada.

Like many large North American cities, Mexico City is beset by some of the worst traffic, smog, and pollution that is found anywhere in the world. It is estimated that Mexico City's three million cars cause three-quarters of the nation's pollution. Some estimates even indicate that the city's car emissions spew 12,000 tons of pollutants into the air daily. Health alerts indicating that pollution has reached dangerous levels are a regular feature of life in the Mexican capital. Like Mexico City, Los Angeles is another city also plagued by smog.

Above *Crumbling buildings stand beside gleaming skyscapers in the center of New York City. Many U.S. city centers are riddled with poverty and crime, as those who can afford it have moved out to the suburbs.*

INDEPENDENCE FOR QUEBEC?

In Canada the issue of separatism is an ongoing dilemma. Quebec residents are staunchly proud of their province and their French heritage. For decades many of the French-speaking citizens of Quebec have sought independence. In 1995 voters in Quebec narrowly defeated a resolution that would have made Canada's most populous and prosperous province an independent nation. Quebec's economy is large enough to give it a rank in the world economy equal to that of some of the smaller European nations.

Left *The "Crusade for Canada" march on October 27, 1995, when 20,000 people marched to persuade the people of Quebec to vote against seceding from Canada.*

THE CHANGING WORKPLACE

Today, advances in different technologies are leading to changes in the workplace for many North Americans. In some places, heavy manufacturing industries have been replaced by the computer and service industries. Those who can have moved to take advantage of these new job opportunities.

In other regions, especially Mexico but also Central America and the Caribbean, new manufacturing industries have grown up. These are often based around large U.S. firms that have relocated in search of reduced production costs. People have changed from an agricultural way of life to an industrial one.

URBAN DECAY

Many urban areas throughout the continent have been especially hard hit by the growth of the suburban and rural shopping malls. Here, under one roof, shoppers can find everything they need, plus dining and entertainment facilities. In most cases, all people need is a car to get them there. Statistics show that some 86 percent of U.S. workers use cars to get to work each day. Wealthy suburbs have grown up as downtown city centers have become deserted—potential sites for poverty and crime. And although statistics released in early 1996 show that there has been a drop in violent crimes in cities of more than one million people, most residents remain insecure and downright afraid of walking city streets alone after dark.

THE CHALLENGE FOR THE FUTURE

The greatest challenge confronting North America is to raise the standard of living of its poorest people. Many of the continent's difficulties would be eased if this can happen. Illegal immigration, crime in the inner cities, and the drug trade all have their roots in poverty, and a slight increase in the wealth of the poorest people could have a dramatic effect on solving each of these problems.

Below *Children in Guaymas, Mexico, carry banners asking people to look after the environment.*

TIME LINE

B.C.

75,000–10,000 The first Americans—ice age hunters from Siberia—cross a land bridge into North America from Asia.

1150 The Olmec civilization spreads from the Mexican areas that are now southern Veracruz and Tabasco.

300 B.C.–A.D. 100 The Maya of Guatemala and the Yucatán Peninsula develop one of the greatest civilizations of the Western Hemisphere.

A.D.

1000–1200 The Toltec Empire dominates the Valley of Mexico.

1400 The Aztec Empire, centered on the great city of Tenochtitlán, dominates. Today's Mexico City stands on the site of Tenochtitlán.

1492 Columbus's ship lands on Watling Island in the Bahamas.

1500s Spanish conquistadors, priests, and settlers build a huge empire in Central and Southern America, Mexico, Texas, and the Caribbean.

1600s Great Britain, France, Holland, and Russia all begin colonies in northern North America.

1620 Pilgrims arrive in Massachusetts from Great Britain.

1756–63 French and Indian wars leave British in charge of most of North America.

1775–83 The American Revolution: local discontent at the way Great Britain runs its North American colonies leads to a war between colonists and British forces.

1776 July 4: Colonial Congress signs the Declaration of Independence from Great Britain.

1803 Louisiana Territory purchased from France by U.S. government, doubling the United States's land area.

1821 Mexico and the Central American countries are all independent from Spain by this time.

1846–48 California won from Spain during the Mexican War.

1861–65 Civil War, over the outlawing of slavery, between southern and northern states.

1867 U.S. government purchases Alaska from Russia.

1898 Spanish-American War.

1914–18 World War I: Canadians join British forces in Europe. U.S. economy booms through selling goods to European countries during the war. United States joins the war in 1917, on the side of Great Britain and France.

1926 Canada becomes independent from Great Britain, while retaining strong ties to the British government.

1929 Wall Street Crash leads to the Great Depression. Collapse of U.S. economy leads other countries into depression as well.

1939–45 World War II sparks a demand for U.S.-produced goods and U.S. economy booms. Commonwealth forces join Great Britain in war in 1939; the United States enters the war in late 1941, after Japan bombs the U.S. naval base at Pearl Harbor, Hawaii. The war ends when U.S. forces drop atomic bombs on the Japanese cities of Hiroshima and Nagasaki.

1950–53 Korean War: the United States sends forces to support anticommunist troops in Korea. Other countries, including Great Britain, also lend support.

1952 Fulgencio Batista seizes power in Cuba and begins a dictatorship.

1956 Fidel Castro begins a guerilla war in Cuba against Batista's dictatorship.

1959: January 1 Batista flees Cuba: Castro takes power and begins a program of nationalization. Over $1 billion of U.S.-owned properties are seized by the new government.

1962 United States declares export embargo on Cuba. USSR places nuclear missiles in Cuba, causing a confrontation between the United States and the USSR. Eventually, the USSR leader, Kruschchev, orders the withdrawal of the missiles.

1964–73 U.S. forces support anticommunist forces in Vietnam's civil war. China, Vietnam's northern neighbor and a communist country, supports the communist forces, and the conflict escalates. During the war "draft dodgers"— young men who don't want to be forced into fighting in Vietnam—escape to Canada or go underground in the United States, moving from place to place to escape the authorities. Protests at home and heavy losses in the war force a U.S. withdrawal in 1973.

1982 Canada ends formal legislative links with Great Britain, by obtaining the right to amend its own constitution.

1983 October Military coup in Haiti ousts Maurice Bishop, the prime minister. Bishop is freed by his supporters, then rearrested by military and hanged. United States invades Grenada: military occupation continues until 1985.

1987 Meech Lake Agreement, giving Quebec special protection for French language and culture, is rejected in Canada. The rejection sparks a separatist movement in Quebec.

1992 Charlottetown Agreement, recognizing Quebec as a "distinct society" and giving native peoples the right to self-government, is defeated in a national referendum.

1994 The North American Free Trade Agreement (NAFTA), between Canada, the United States, and Mexico, comes into effect. The agreement allows free trade of goods between the three countries.

GLOSSARY

Civilization An identifiable culture that dominates a whole region, sometimes in more than one country.

Climate The temperature and rainfall that is most common in a region is its climate. A place that is generally cold is said to have a cold climate, even though some days might be quite warm; somewhere with very little rain throughout the year has a dry climate.

Commonwealth An independent state or community, or an interdependent group of states. Great Britain and the countries that were once part of its empire, for example, now make up a commonwealth.

Confederation An alliance, usually a fairly permanent one, of different states under one government.

Emigrate To leave your own country to go and live in another.

Empire A group of countries, colonies, or settlements under the control of a more powerful government. For example, the Aztecs of Mexico began to take control of lands surrounding their own in the 14th century: the whole of the area became known as the Aztec Empire.

Glacier A buildup of ice and snow that grinds down a valley, carrying rocks and soil along with it. As more snow and ice accumulate at the top of the valley, the glacier moves forward under the weight of material behind it.

Hispanic Based on the influence and traditions of Spain, or of Spanish ancestry or origin.

Immigrant A person from another country who comes to live in a new country.

Isthmus A narrow strip of land that connects two larger land areas.

Industrialized Describing an economy based on manufacturing or processing of resources rather than agriculture, as the main source of work.

Literacy rates The proportion of people who can read.

Mestizo People of mixed European and Indian descent.

Norseman A man from Scandinavia, where Nordic (or Norse) languages are spoken.

Peninsula A piece of land nearly surrounded by water.

Plateau A raised, flat, or nearly flat area of land.

Republic A system of government in which all the rulers are elected by the people.

Seceding Withdrawing from an organization, such as a political party or federation.

Separatist An advocate of independence or autonomy for a part of a political unit, such as a nation.

Smallpox A disease that causes a terrible fever, large spots that scar the skin, and often death.

Tariff A set of duties imposed by a government on imported or exported goods.

Tundra Lands without any trees, where all but the top layer of soil is frozen.

Typhus A disease that causes purple spots, a terrible fever, coughing, and often death.

FURTHER READING

Nonfiction

Anderson, Marcie. *Exploring the Fifty States*. St. Petersburg, FL: Willowisp Press, 1994.

Ayer, Elizabeth. *Canada*. World Partners. Vero Beach, FL: Rourke Corp., 1990.

Baines, John D. *The U.S.A.* Country Fact Files. Austin, TX: Raintree Steck-Vaughn, 1993.

Brill, Marlene T. & Targ, Harry R. *Guatemala*. Enchantment of the World. Danbury, CT: Children's Press, 1993.

Department of Geography, Lerner Publications. *Mexico in Pictures*. Visual Geography. Minneapolis, MN: Lerner Group, 1994.

Hartley, Nancy. *Quick Facts about the U.S.A.* New York: Scholastic, 1995.

Kott, Jennifer. *Nicaragua*. Cultures of the World. Tarrytown, NY: Marshall Cavendish, 1994.

Malcolm, Andrew H. *The Land & People of Canada*. Portraits of the Nations. New York: HarperCollins Children's Books, 1991.

Reilly, Mary J. *Mexico*. Cultures of the World. Tarrytown, NY: Marshall Cavendish, 1991.

Reimers, David M. *A Land of Immigrants*. Immigrant Experience. New York: Chelsea House, 1995.

Rummel, Jack. *Mexico*. Let's Visit Places & Peoples of the World. New York: Chelsea House, 1990.

Stein, R. Conrad. *The United States of America*. Enchantment of the World. Danbury, CT: Children's Press, 1994.

Stefoff, Rebecca. *Independence and Revolution in Mexico, 1810–1940*. World History Library. New York: Facts on File, 1993.

Wright, David K. *Canada*. Children of the World. Milwaukee, WI: Gareth Stevens, 1991.

Atlases are also a good source of information about countries. Most modern encyclopedias, especially those on CD-ROM, are a useful source of information on North America.

Novels
There are many great American writers, far too many to list here. Among the most famous American novels are
Moby Dick by Herman Melville
Huckleberry Finn by Mark Twain
Uncle Tom's Cabin by Harriet Beecher Stowe

More recent novels from North America include *Solomon Gursky Was Here* by Mordecai Richler, which is set in the northern wastes of Canada; the books of Robertson Davies, especially *The Deptford Trilogy*, the story of a friendship between two boys, one of whom grows up to become the world's most famous magician; and *Miguel Street* by V. S. Naipaul, about a young boy's childhood in Trinidad.

INDEX